SOUTH CAROLINA
The Palmetto State

★

TEN TOP FACTS ABOUT SOUTH CAROLINA

★ ★ ★ ★ ★ ★ ★ ★ ★ ★ ★ ★ ★

•State nicknames: The Palmetto State

•State mottoes: *Animis Opibusque Parati* (Latin for "Prepared in Mind and Resources") and *Dum Spiro Spero* (Latin for "While I Breathe, I Hope")

•Capital: Columbia

•Area: 31,113 square miles

•State flower: Yellow jessamine

•State tree: Palmetto

•State bird: Carolina wren

•State insect: Carolina mantis

•State dance: The Shag

•State songs: "Carolina" and "South Carolina on My Mind"

This is for Patrick Price, my brother and favorite
South Carolinian.

Photo credits:

p. 4: U.S. Mint; p. 5: North Wind Picture Archives, Alfred, ME; p. 6: (bottom left and right) North Wind Picture Archives; p. 7: North Wind Picture Archives; p. 8: (top right) Brown Brothers, Sterling, PA, (bottom) North Wind Picture Archives; p. 9: (top and center left) North Wind Picture Archives, (bottom) Superstock Images, Jacksonville, FL; p. 10: (both) North Wind Picture Archives; p. 11: (bottom left) North Wind Picture Archives, (bottom right) Library of Congress, Washington, D.C.; p. 12: (top left) North Wind Picture Archives, (others) Bettmann/Corbis, New York, NY; p. 13: (top left) North Wind Picture Archives, (bottom) Brown Brothers; p. 14: Corbis; p. 15: AP/Wide World Photos, Inc.; p. 16: (left) Bettmann/Corbis, (top right) South Carolina Department of Parks, Recreation and Tourism, Columbia, SC, (bottom right) Superstock Images; p. 17: South Carolina Department of Parks, Recreation and Tourism; p. 18: (top right) Bettmann/Corbis, (bottom) J. McLear/Transparencies, Inc.; p. 19: (top left) Superstock Images, (top right) South Carolina Department of Parks, Recreation and Tourism, (center right) R. Gehman/Corbis; p. 20: (left) Superstock Images, (top right) South Carolina Department of Parks, Recreation and Tourism, (bottom right) W. Bake/Corbis; p. 21: (top left) Superstock Images, (bottom left) Historic Columbia Foundation, Columbia, SC, (right) South Carolina Department of Parks, Recreation and Tourism; p. 22: Library of Congress (Bethune), AP/Wide World Photos (Frazier), Brown Brothers (Gibson and Heyward); p. 23: Superstock Images (Andrew Jackson) AP/Wide World Photos (Jesse Jackson), Bettmann/Corbis (Joe Jackson), North Wind Picture Archives (Smalls); p. 24: The South Caroliniana Library, University of South Carolina, Columbia, SC.

Photo research by Dwayne Howard

All other illustrations by John Speirs.

ISBN 0-439-22289-3

12 11 10 9 8 7 6 5 4 3 2 1   1 2 3 4 5/0

Designed by Madalina Stefan

Printed in the U.S.A.

First Scholastic printing, April 2001

SOUTH CAROLINA
The Palmetto State

By Sean Stewart Price

SCHOLASTIC INC.

New York Toronto London Auckland Sydney Mexico City New Delhi Hong Kong

A Celebration of the Fifty States

★ ★ ★ ★ ★ ★ ★ ★ ★ ★ ★ ★

In January 1999, the U.S. Mint started an ambitious ten-year program to commemorate each of the fifty United States. Over the next several years (through 2008), they will issue five newly designed quarters each year.

One side (obverse) of each new quarter will display the profile of George Washington and the words *Liberty, In God We Trust,* and *United States of America.* The other side (reverse) will feature a design honoring a specific state's unique history, the year it became a state, the year of the quarter's issue, and the words *E Pluribus Unum* (Latin for "from many, one"). The quarters are being issued in the order in which the states joined the union, beginning with the thirteen original colonies.

To find out more about the 50 State Quarters™ Program, visit the official U.S. Mint Web site at *www.usmint.gov.*

SOUTH CAROLINA'S QUARTER:
The Mighty Palmetto Tree

On June 28, 1776, cannonballs were flying in Charleston Harbor. On one side were the British redcoats, determined to take the city and stop the American Revolution. On the other side were defiant South Carolinians protected by a fort made of palmetto logs. The British ships fired time after time into the tough, spongy logs. But their cannonballs did little damage, and the Americans won a great battle.

On that day, a blue flag with a crescent moon flew over the American fort. South Carolinians later added a palmetto tree to their state flag and adopted the nickname "The Palmetto State." South Carolina's quarter features the palmetto tree along with the Carolina wren, the state bird, and the yellow jessamine, the state flower. It also includes an outline of the state with a star marking the capital city, Columbia.

Early settlers

Discovering Paradise

The first Europeans to see South Carolina during the 1500s and 1600s called it a Garden of Eden. A person could walk for miles through dense forests of soaring oaks and pines. Turkeys, beavers, and panthers roamed the woods, while catfish, bass, and alligators swam in the rivers and swamps.

At the time, South Carolina was home to about thirty Native American tribes. Most Indians relied on farming, but men also had to be keen hunters. Among the biggest tribes were the Cherokee, who lived in the mountainous western part of the state; the Catawba, who lived in the northern foothills; and the Yamasee, who lived along the southern coast.

Starting in 1521, both Spain and France tried to set up colonies in the region. Both failed, however, due to starvation,

Indian attacks, and sickness. In spite of their unsuccessful attempts to colonize, the Europeans managed to harm the Indians by bringing diseases such as smallpox and yellow fever to the New World. The Native Americans had no immunity against these illnesses. In 1540, Spanish explorer Hernando de Soto found that whole Indian villages in South Carolina had been wiped out by epidemics.

Carolana to Carolina

In 1629, British King Charles I claimed a large chunk of land in what is today the southeastern United States. The land was originally called *Carolana,* a Latin word that means the "land of Charles," and it included what is now North Carolina and South Carolina as one territory. The spelling was later

5

changed to *Carolina,* and the colony was divided into two colonies — north and south — in 1712.

In 1663, the king's son, Charles II, handed control of South Carolina over to eight English noblemen called the "lords proprietors." They sent the first British settlers to the region, a group of about 130 men and women, in March 1670. Those settlers landed at Albemarle Point and called the area Charles Towne, after their king. Ten years later, the settlement moved about three miles away to a skinny peninsula between the Ashley and the Cooper rivers. The city founded there gradually became known as "Charlestown" during colonial days. It was officially renamed Charleston in 1783. Today, it is South Carolina's largest and most important urban area and port.

Though disease had reduced the number of Indians by as much as one-third, there were still tens of thousands of them living in South Carolina. As more European settlers arrived, they pushed Indians off their lands, and bloody wars broke out. In 1715, the Yamasee tribe and its allies almost destroyed the young colony. European colonists finally drove the Yamasee into Spanish-held Florida, but South Carolina was in ruins.

Pirate ship

Indians were not the only threat to the colony. Pirates raided South Carolina's coast many times. In 1717, the infamous pirate Blackbeard sailed into Charleston Harbor and threatened to kill hostages if he did not get medical supplies. Blackbeard's demands were met and the hostages were saved. The next year, Blackbeard was killed after a fierce sea battle off North Carolina's coast. South Carolinians hunted down several other pirates, too, and those not killed in battle were usually hanged.

Indians attacking a South Carolina plantation

The pirate Blackbeard

6

Slaves unloading rice from barges

The Road to Independence

The lord proprietors lived far away and did little to protect South Carolina from pirates, Indians, and other threats. In 1719, the colonists rebelled by ignoring the proprietors' officials and choosing their own representatives. They demanded to become a royal colony controlled directly by England's King George I. Becoming a royal colony gave South Carolinians far more power over their own affairs.

South Carolina thrived during this period. The area along the coast, called the Low Country, became the site of rich plantations. These giant farms relied on slaves brought from Africa to harvest crops like rice and indigo (a blue dye used in clothing). Areas farther inland became known as the Up Country. Immigrants from Europe and other colonies caused the Up Country's population to swell. Most people there had only small farms. They could not afford slaves and had little in common with the wealthy plantation owners from the Low Country.

During the French and Indian War (1756–1763), Great Britain battled France and its Indian allies for control of North America. In South Carolina, the war set off bloody battles between Up Country settlers and the Cherokee that did not end until 1761. The British won the war, but at great cost. In the 1760s, they passed a series of taxes and restrictive trade laws that greatly angered American colonists. For instance, the Stamp Act of 1765 taxed all paper items from legal documents to newspapers. It imposed a heavy tax burden and caused riots in Charleston. The Stamp Act was repealed, but was then replaced by other offensive laws such as the Townsend Act of 1767 (which taxed paper, glass, and other items), and the Quartering Act of 1774 (which allowed British soldiers to take over private homes).

The colonists' unrest led to the start of the Revolutionary War on April 19, 1775, with the Battles of Lexington and Concord in Massachusetts. At the time, most South Carolinians still opposed independence from Britain. Many, called Tories, were still loyal to Great Britain, while others simply feared making a break with the greatest empire on Earth. But the momentum for independence was unstoppable. In July 1776, South Carolina representatives Thomas Heyward Jr., Thomas Lynch Jr., Arthur Middleton, and Edward Rutledge signed the Declaration of Independence at the Second Continental Congress in Philadelphia.

Just a week before the Declaration of Independence was signed, South Carolina won one of the biggest victories of the revolution. British warships tried to capture Charleston, the most important port city in the South. American General

William Moultrie led the defense of Charleston Harbor and beat back the British with heavy losses. Such a badly needed victory raised the hopes of the patriots in their struggle for independence.

For four years, South Carolina saw little violence. Then, in April 1780, the British came back and captured Charleston and 5,500 patriots. That terrible blow was followed by an even more stunning British victory at Camden in August, which all but destroyed the Continental army in the South. After that battle, the patriot cause saw its darkest hour.

British attack on Fort Moultrie

At about the same time, South Carolina guerrilla leaders like General Francis Marion, the "Swamp Fox," and General Thomas Sumter, the "Gamecock," began harassing the redcoats. Their small, mobile bands

Thomas Sumter

made lightning-swift attacks that kept the British off balance. Two months after the defeat at Camden, patriots at Kings Mountain crushed an army of Tories. In

Battle of Kings Mountain

January 1781, General Daniel Morgan defeated the British again at Cowpens. In all, about two hundred battles and skirmishes took place in South Carolina, more than in any other colony.

The British finally marched out of Charleston in 1782, and the war ended a year later, leaving South Carolina devastated. Its economy was in terrible shape, and people from the Low Country and the Up Country felt deep bitterness toward one another. Violence occasionally flared between the two sides, and it took many years for tensions to die down. In 1786, South Carolina moved its state capital to Columbia — in the middle of the state — in an effort to make it more accessible to the entire population and less likely to be dominated by the wealthy plantation owners near Charleston.

As the state mended and rebuilt, its leaders played an important role in writing the U.S. Constitution. South Carolina sent four men to the 1787 Constitutional Convention in Philadelphia — Pierce Butler, Charles Cotesworth Pickney, Charles Pickney, and John Rutledge. Charles Pickney had an especially strong influence. His proposals helped define the President's duties and even introduced the title "President." On May 23, 1788, South Carolina ratified the document and became the eighth state to enter the union.

Battle of Cowpens

Slaves picking and baling cotton

King Cotton

In 1793, the invention of a machine called the cotton gin radically changed South Carolina. Just one gin could remove more cotton seeds than fifty laborers. That allowed plantation owners to grow and sell cotton more easily. To do that, they needed lots of African slaves to plant and pick their crops. South Carolina had always depended upon slaves. Now, though, the demand for slaves soared.

Throughout the early 1800s, "King Cotton" took over the South's economy. As it did, South Carolina's society developed into four main groups.

Planters: This small group of plantation owners controlled the state's government and wealth. Most of them lived in the Low Country in and around Charleston. But the invention of the cotton gin spread plantations all over the state. Because of their rich lifestyle and high-handed ways, planters were often compared to English aristocrats.

Plain folks: The majority of white South Carolinians were poor people who owned no slaves. They tended to be farmers from the Up Country, but many had occupations such as blacksmith, wagon maker, and shop owner.

Using a cotton gin

Blacksmiths at work

Free blacks: These people made up only two percent of the population. Though free, they had few rights. The most famous free black was a Charleston carpenter named Denmark Vesey. In 1822, Vesey organized the largest slave revolt in U.S. history. He and his followers planned to seize weapons, free hundreds of slaves,

10

board ships in the harbor, and sail to a friendly country. However, Vesey was betrayed by a slave before he could act. He and twenty-one others were hanged.

Slaves: For most of the time between 1690 and 1920, blacks greatly outnumbered whites in South Carolina. That is because the state's giant plantations needed thousands of slaves to pick cotton, rice, and other crops. Many South Carolina blacks, both free and slave, spoke a language called Gullah. It evolved among the slaves from a combination of their African languages. English words like *goober* (peanut) and *tote* (to carry) come from Gullah.

Rising Tensions

In the 1830s, South Carolina planters became furious when Congress created taxes that hurt the demand for cotton overseas. Growing antislavery feelings in the North also angered planters. Led by Senator John C. Calhoun, South Carolina declared that the taxes were "nullified," meaning that the state didn't have to pay them. South Carolina's leaders even threatened to secede (or leave) the Union. In reply, President Andrew Jackson threatened to send U.S. troops to South Carolina.

Congress finally lowered the taxes, and South Carolina backed down. However, the nullification crisis led

Abraham Lincoln

to greater tensions between North and South. By 1860, those tensions had split the entire country apart. Abraham Lincoln, who opposed the practice of slavery, was elected President that November. The idea of having an antislavery President in the White House horrified Southerners. On December 20, 1860, South Carolina passed an ordinance stating:

"We the people of the State of South Carolina in Convention assembled, do declare and ordain . . . that the union now [existing] between South Carolina and the other States, under the name of the 'United States of America' is hereby dissolved."

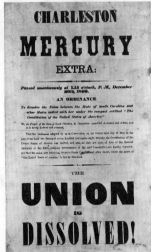

Newspaper headline announcing the dissolution of the United States

Attack on Fort Sumter

The Civil War

South Carolina's secession from the Union prompted ten other Southern states to leave. Together they formed the Confederate States of America. On April 12, 1861, Confederate troops opened fire on Fort Sumter in Charleston Harbor, the first shots of the Civil War.

Most South Carolinians were confident of victory, and more than 60,000 of them marched off to fight. A Union naval blockade, however, soon stopped all trade with foreign countries, choking off basic supplies like cloth and flour. On February 17, 1864, the Confederate submarine *Hunley* sank the Union blockade ship *Housatonic* in Charleston. It was the first

General William T. Sherman

successful submarine attack in history, but it failed to end the blockade.

By the winter of 1865, the Confederacy had suffered great losses but refused to give up. In February, Union General William T. Sherman captured Atlanta, Georgia, marched his huge army to the sea, then went back through South Carolina to the city of Columbia. Union troops wanted to take revenge for the state's leadership in the Confederate cause. "I almost tremble at her fate," Sherman said as he began his march. His army left a path of destruction thirty miles wide.

On April 9, 1865, Confederate General Robert E. Lee surrendered at Appomattox, Virginia, and the war ended. By that time, South Carolina was shattered. Its economy and society, which depended on cotton and slaves, had been destroyed. About one-fifth of South Carolina's fighting men were killed in the war, and thousands of others were wounded.

General Sherman's troops on their march through South Carolina

Freed slaves
leaving a plantation

After the War

The years after the war were difficult for South Carolina. More than 400,000 slaves rejoiced to find themselves free. For the first time, they could vote and hold public office. At the state's 1868 constitutional convention, 73 of the 124 delegates were African-American. As time passed, though, white terrorist groups like the Ku Klux Klan used violence to scare away black voters. In 1895, Senator Ben

Tillman pushed to make South Carolina a Jim Crow state. ("Jim Crow" was a derogatory name for black people.) Jim Crow laws enforced segregation and robbed blacks of many basic rights, such as the right to vote and to serve on a jury.

The war and its aftermath made South Carolina extremely poor. Most people still farmed, raising cotton and tobacco. By 1900, hundreds of mills that made yarn and cloth moved to the state. Children as young as eight years old worked in the mills with adults. All millworkers had to endure brutal twelve-hour days. One of them remembered, "The farmer can sit by his fire all day when it freezes, rains, or snows, but we got to go to the mill every day, just the same."

Children working in a mill

Good Times and Bad

South Carolina prospered during World War I (1914–1918) because demand for cotton and cloth soared. In the 1920s, however, an insect called the boll weevil chewed up half the state's cotton crop. Many farmers were ruined. Things got worse in 1929 when the Great Depression left one in four Americans out of work. South Carolina was hit especially hard. Throughout the early 1900s, tens of thousands of people, both black and white, left the state.

Boll weevil on a cotton plant

Strangely, South Carolina's long spell of hard times had a hidden benefit. Many of the old buildings from the early 1800s still stood. Few people had the money to replace them. As a result, wealthy tourists took an interest in the state's history. Charleston, with its old run-down mansions, suddenly became a hot tourist spot in the late 1920s. In the coming decades, the city once again became wealthy and powerful.

However, it took World War II (1939–1945) to bring South Carolina into the modern age. Government spending on weapons, military bases, and other items pumped money into the state and created jobs. Hydroelectric dams built during and after the war helped bring electricity to farm areas and attracted out-of-state industries. South Carolina gradually became less dependent upon cloth mills and farms to make money.

Sharecropper's family during the Great Depression

Segregated train station

Civil Rights

After World War II, South Carolina had to face the problems created by its Jim Crow laws. Blacks were not allowed to enter the same restaurants, stores, or theaters as whites. They were also forced to attend separate, poorly funded schools. It cost much more to keep the two races apart than it would have to educate everyone together. As one college official put it in 1954, "The price of prejudice is very high."

That same year, the U.S. Supreme Court ruled that having separate schools for blacks and whites was unconstitutional. For many years, white South Carolinians dug in their heels, refusing to integrate schools and other facilities. Blacks demonstrated peacefully against such discrimination. A South Carolina folk song called "We Shall Overcome" became the anthem for civil rights protesters throughout the South.

In the 1960s, racial segregation finally fell apart. Federal laws passed in 1964 and 1965 ended the Jim Crow system, allowing blacks to vote once again. South Carolina's transition from segregation to integration was mostly peaceful, but racial tensions still remain today. In 1963, South Carolina began flying the Confederate battle flag over its state capitol. The flag was finally taken down in the summer of 2000 after a long, nationally publicized debate. Supporters of the flag argued that it reflected southern pride, while opponents said it was racist and a symbol of rebellion.

South Carolina Today

South Carolina has changed tremendously since the days of Jim Crow. Farms still produce crops such as tobacco, peaches, soybeans, and corn. But the state's population exploded after 1970, and industry, not farming, is now the chief moneymaker. Cloth mills remain important, but South Carolinians today are more likely to earn a living by managing a store or building cars.

South Carolina often makes headlines because of its hurricanes. On September 21, 1989, Hurricane Hugo became the tenth-most ferocious storm to hit the United States during the twentieth century. It killed 180 people while wiping out at least 40,000 homes. Hugo's eye, or center, passed near Charleston, packing winds of up to 130 miles per hour. It took many years for the city to recover.

Buildings destroyed by Hurricane Hugo

No matter how many storms batter South Carolina, it manages to keep rebuilding and remaking itself. One hundred years ago, it was a poor state that was often overlooked by outsiders. Today, it is an international crossroads. Charleston helped lead the way by creating the Spoleto Festival in 1977. Each May, the city runs an exchange program with artists from the city of Spoleto, Italy. The result is an extravaganza of music, theater, dance, art, and film events. More than 22,000 people from all over the world come to Charleston just to enjoy the festival.

Spoleto Festival

In fact, tourism has become the biggest industry in the Low Country. Areas like Charleston, Hilton Head Island, and Myrtle Beach draw hundreds of thousands of visitors each year. The same natural beauty and sunny climate that made early pioneers call South Carolina a Garden of Eden attract a new kind of explorer today.

Myrtle Beach

16

Charleston today

The "Charleston" and the "Shag"

In the Roaring 1920s, just about every young person in the United States knew how to dance the Charleston. It was a lively dance step with lots of kicking and hand waving. Some believe the Charleston got started among black musicians in Charleston itself. Whatever its origins, the Charleston became a hit with the teenage crowd, thanks to a 1923 Broadway musical called *Runnin' Wild*.

Another dance, called the Shag, is also said to have originated in South Carolina. The Shag, a fast dance originally performed to big band music in the 1930s and 1940s, then to rhythm and blues, and finally to rock and roll, has been *the* dance of the Carolina beach scene for years. In fact, South Carolina made it the official state dance in 1984. Today, the Myrtle Beach area remains the heart of Shag-dancing country, with clubs and dance contests all around the region.

Dancing the Charleston

Dancing the Shag

Things to Do and Places to See

John Calhoun's mansion

Charles Towne Landing

Charleston

The city of Charleston and its 300-year-old 1,000-acre historic district are popular tourist attractions. The past truly comes alive in this city. Grand old houses like the Calhoun Mansion and the Miles Brewton House offer tours, while historic monuments like Fort Sumter, named after Revolutionary War hero Thomas Sumter, cater to Civil War buffs. It also has a world-class aquarium overlooking Charleston Harbor. The Spoleto Festival in May is just one of many cultural events that make the city fascinating.

Charles Towne Landing

This living-history park gives visitors an idea of what South Carolina's first English settlers faced in the late 1600s. It is located on Charleston's original site, about ten miles away from the present city. The remains of the fort have been preserved. There is also a museum and a replica of a trading ship from colonial times.

Bald cypress trees in Congaree Swamp

Congaree Swamp National Monument

When the first settlers arrived in South Carolina, much of what they found was swampland. Most of the swamps have disappeared over the centuries, except for this 15,000-acre park just southeast of

Columbia. People can canoe or hike through 18 miles of trails to explore this unusual and beautiful area.

Marina on Hilton Head Island

Hilton Head Island

Once home to cotton plantations, this beautiful island is now a hot vacation spot. Hilton Head boasts twelve miles of beaches, twenty-seven golf courses, more than 300 tennis courts, three protected wildlife habitats, several historic sites, and plenty of room to bicycle or in-line skate.

Historic Brattonsville District

Historic Brattonsville is a complex of homes and structures dating from the 1700s and 1800s. It is located near Rock Hill on the site of a plantation that once housed 180 people, most of them slaves. Summer camps here show children old-fashioned skills, such as how to cook over an open fire. Brattonsville has also been used by

Historic Brattonsville

filmmakers looking to recreate the colonial and pre-Civil War eras.

Kings Mountain National Military Park and Cowpens National Battlefield

Kings Mountain and Cowpens were the sites of two of the most important victories of the American Revolution. In October 1780, the Continental army defeated the British at Kings Mountain. Four months later, a British force was wiped out at Cowpens, and from then on, the colonists remained in the lead. These two battlefields, located near Rock Hill, are about a half-hour drive from each other. Aside from their historic interest, both battlefields offer

Monument at Cowpens National Battlefield

hiking, biking, and picnic areas nearby. Kings Mountain State Park, right next to the battlefield, has areas for camping, swimming, and fishing.

Magnolia Gardens

Magnolia Plantation and Gardens

This world-famous plantation near Charleston has been owned by the same family — the Draytons — since the 1680s. The original house was burned down by Union troops during the Civil War, but the rebuilt mansion is only part of the attraction. There is also a tropical garden, a wildlife refuge, and a petting zoo. For the adventurous individual, there is a garden maze to get lost in and the Audubon Swamp Garden to explore.

Mann-Simons Cottage

Mann-Simons Cottage: Museum of African-American Culture

In 1860, a Charleston slave named Celia Mann bought her freedom and walked 112 miles to Columbia. She took up residence in this humble cottage, which now helps show visitors how ordinary people — both black and white — lived in the 1800s.

Gardens at Middleton Place

Middleton Place

Middleton Place, just northwest of Charleston, is a reminder of how grand and how destructive South Carolina's history has been. Originally, it was the home of Henry Middleton, president of the first Continental Congress and a signer of the Declaration of Independence. Before the Civil War, the mansion was one of the finest in the South. Its beautiful gardens and butterfly-shaped lakes are still impressive. However, in February 1865, Union troops burned down most of the mansion. The only surviving wing was rebuilt, and today serves as a museum.

Famous People from South Carolina

Mary McLeod Bethune (1875–1955)

Bethune was a key civil rights and women's rights leader in the early 1900s. A child of slaves, she grew up near Mayesville, picking cotton. In 1904, Bethune set up her own school in Florida, which today is Bethune-Cookman College. In 1936, President Franklin D. Roosevelt named her director of the Division of Negro Affairs in the National Youth Administration. That made Bethune the first black woman to head a federal agency.

Althea Gibson (1927–)

Althea Gibson was born in a town called Silver. On August 25, 1950, she became the first black tennis player to play in the tournament now known as the U.S. Open. A year later she became the first black American to play at Wimbledon in England. Gibson's participation in those tournaments destroyed the color barrier in professional tennis. In 1957, Gibson became the first black woman to win the singles titles at both the U.S. Open and Wimbledon.

Joe Frazier (1944–)

Joe Frazier's parents were poor cotton farmers from Beaufort. As a boy, Frazier trained to be a boxer using a homemade punching bag. In 1964, he became the first U.S. heavyweight to win the gold medal in Olympic boxing. From 1970 to 1973, he reigned as the undefeated world heavyweight champion. Between 1971 and 1975, he fought three famous matches against Muhammad Ali, winning once and losing twice. In 1990, Frazier was inducted into the International Boxing Hall of Fame.

DuBose Heyward (1885–1940)

In 1925, Charleston author DuBose Heyward wrote the book *Porgy* about a group of poor black Charlestonians. Nine years later, he helped the famous songwriting team of George and Ira Gershwin turn his story into an opera called *Porgy and Bess*. Heyward helped write the words to several songs for the work, including "Summertime." *Porgy and Bess* remains the most popular American opera in the world.

Andrew Jackson (1767–1845)

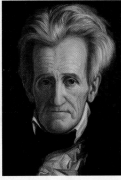

Andrew Jackson was born near the border of North Carolina and South Carolina, and both states often claim him as a native. Called "Old Hickory" because of his toughness, Jackson became a national hero during the War of 1812 when his army crushed the British in the Battle of New Orleans. Jackson later helped found the Democratic party and was elected President in 1828. His influence was so strong that the following two decades are often called the "Age of Jackson."

Jesse Jackson (1941–)

Since the assassination of Martin Luther King Jr. in 1968, Jesse Jackson has been the most prominent African-American in U.S. politics. In 1984 and 1988, Jackson ran to become the Democratic nominee for President. Both campaigns were unsuccessful. However, Jackson, who was born near Greenville, was the first African-American to make a serious run for the White House. He garnered strong support, and his speeches called attention to the plight of less fortunate Americans of all races.

"Shoeless" Joe Jackson (1887–1951)

"Shoeless" Joe Jackson from Brandon Mills was one of the greatest and most tragic players in professional baseball. He got his nickname during a minor-league game when, because of some blisters, he played without shoes. During Jackson's thirteen-year career, he racked up a .356 batting average, the third-highest in major league history. In 1919, he was caught up in the Black Sox scandal. Members of the Chicago White Sox took money from gamblers to deliberately lose the World Series. Though Jackson played brilliantly during the series, he did take the money. Afterward he was banned from the game and baseball's Hall of Fame.

Robert Smalls (1839–1915)

Robert Smalls made one of the most daring escapes of the U.S. Civil War. As a slave, he served as wheelman aboard the Confederate ship *Planter* in Charleston. On the night of May 12, 1862, Smalls and other black crewmen stole the *Planter* and sneaked past the Confederate forts that protected Charleston. Smalls surrendered to Union ships, where he was hailed as a hero. He eventually reached the rank of captain in the U.S. Navy, an unheard-of promotion for a black man at that time. After the war, Smalls became one of South Carolina's first black congressmen.

Mary Chesnut and the Civil War

Mary Chesnut (1823–1886) was a wealthy woman from Camden, South Carolina, who had a ringside seat to the Civil War. Her husband was a Confederate general, and she came from a politically powerful family. Her diary was published after her death and has become a must-read for Civil War buffs.

Chesnut was an unusual woman for her time. She opposed slavery (but, like most Southerners, believed that blacks were inferior) and strongly supported women's rights. Her diaries are interesting for the uniquely Southern attitudes they reveal.

The following excerpts from her diary begin just as South Carolina soldiers are about to open fire on Union troops in Fort Sumter — the opening shots of the war. Chesnut was in Charleston at the time. She and other residents of the city could watch the bombardment from their rooftops.

April 12, 1861

I do not pretend to go to sleep. How can I? If Anderson [the Union commander at Fort Sumter] does not accept terms at four the orders are he shall be fired upon. I count four St. Michael [Church] chimes. I begin to hope. At half-past four, the heavy booming of cannon. I sprang out of bed. And on my knees, prostrate, I prayed as I never prayed before.

April 13, 1861

Not by one word or look can we detect any change in the demeanor of these Negro servants [to news that war has broken out]. Laurence sits at our door, as sleepy and as respectful and as profoundly indifferent. So are they all. They carry it too far. You could not tell that they heard even the awful row that is going on in the bay [the shelling of Fort Sumter], though it is dinning in their ears night and day. And people talk before them as if they were chairs and tables. And they make no sign. Are they stolidly stupid or wiser than we are, silent and strong, biding their time?

July 13, 1861

Yesterday . . . we had a glimpse of war. It was the saddest sight. The memory of it is hard to shake off. Sick soldiers, not wounded. There were quite two hundred (they said) lying about as best they might on the [railroad] platform. . . . These pale, ghastly faces. So here is one of the horrors of war we had not reckoned on.

July 24, 1861

A man riding a beautiful horse joined us. He wore a hat with somehow a military look to it. He sat [on] his horse gracefully, and he was so distinguished at all points that I very much regretted not catching the name as Mrs. Stanard gave it to us. He, however, heard ours and bowed as gracefully as he rode, and the few remarks he made to each of us showed he knew all about us. . . . As he left I said, "Who is it?" eagerly. "You did not know! Why, it is Robert E. Lee . . . the first man of Virginia."

February 11, 1862

Confederate affairs in a blue way. Roanoke taken. Fort Henry on the Tennessee River open to them, and we fear the Mississippi River, too. . . . New [Union] armies, new fleets, swarming and threatening everywhere. We ought to have as good a [view] of ourselves as they have of us, and to be willing to do as much to save ourselves from a nauseous union with them as they are willing to do by way of revengeful coercion in forcing us back. . . . I have nervous chills every day. Bad news is killing me.

Christmas Day, 1863

[Confederate soldiers] dropped in after dinner, without arms, without legs. Von Borcke, who cannot speak because of a wound in his throat. Isabella said, "We have all kinds now but a blind one." Poor fellows. They laugh at wounds and yet can show many a scar.

In February 1865, Union General William T. Sherman marched his huge army across South Carolina, destroying almost everything in its path.

February 23, 1865

Charleston and Wilmington, surrendered. I have no further use for a newspaper. I never want to see another one as long as I live. . . . Rain, rain outside, inside naught but drowning floods of tears. I could not bear it, so I rushed down in that rainstorm to [a friend's house where my husband was visiting]. He met me at the door. "Madam, Columbia [the state capital] is burned to the ground." I bowed my head and sobbed aloud.

April 7, 1865

Richmond [the Confederate capital in Virginia] has fallen, I have no heart to write about it. . . . They are too many for us. Everything is lost in Richmond, even our archives. Blue-black is our horizon.

April 1865

With this storm of woe impending, [I and several friends] snatched a moment of reckless gaiety. . . . We played cards. Then the stories told were so amusing I confess I laughed to the point of tears. I knew the trouble was all out there, but we put it off, kept it out one evening, let it bang at the door as it would.

April 19, 1865

Just now Mr. Clay dashed upstairs, pale as a sheet. "General Lee has capitulated." I saw it reflected in Mary Darby's face before I heard him. She staggered to the table, sat down, and wept aloud. Clay's eyes were not dry. Quite beside herself, Mary shrieked, "Now we belong to Negroes and Yankees!"

June 1865

There are two classes of . . . sufferers in this community: (1) those who say, "If people would only pay me what they owe me!" (2) "If people would only let me alone. I cannot pay them. I could stand it if I had anything to pay debts." Now we belong to both classes. Heavens! What people owe us and will not or cannot pay would settle all our debts ten times over and leave us in easy circumstances for life. But they will not pay. How can they?

Carolina Gold

During colonial times, rice was South Carolina's richest crop and an important source of food. It made many planters so wealthy that it became known as "Carolina gold." Since the early 1900s, rice has become less important economically, but it is still a vital part of any South Carolina table. Make sure an adult helps you with this recipe.

Charleston Rice

Ingredients:

½ cup chopped onion
½ cup chopped celery
½ cup chopped green bell pepper
1 tablespoon butter or margarine
3 cups cooked rice (cooked in chicken broth)
1 2½-ounce can mushrooms, drained and chopped

½ teaspoon poultry seasoning
½ teaspoon salt
¼ teaspoon celery seed
¼ teaspoon ground black pepper
1 egg, beaten

Cook the onion, celery, and green pepper in butter in a large skillet over medium heat until tender. Add rice, mushrooms, poultry seasoning, salt, celery seed, and black pepper; stir in the egg. Turn into greased shallow 1½–quart baking dish. Cover and bake at 350°F for 15 minutes.
Makes 4–6 servings.
(Courtesy of the USA Rice Federation)

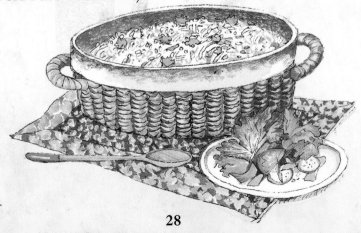